Dominoes

Emma

OXFORD

UNIVERSITY PRESS

Great Clarendon Street, Oxford OX2 6DP

Oxford University Press is a department of the University of Oxford.
It furthers the University's objective of excellence in research, scholarship,
and education by publishing worldwide in

Oxford New York

Auckland Bangkok Buenos Aires Cape Town Chennai
Dar es Salaam Delhi Hong Kong Istanbul Karachi Kolkata
Kuala Lumpur Madrid Melbourne Mexico City Mumbai Nairobi
São Paulo Shanghai Taipei Tokyo Toronto

OXFORD and OXFORD ENGLISH are registered trade marks of
Oxford University Press

ISBN 0 19 424345 1

© Oxford University Press 2002

First published 2002
Third impression 2003

A complete recording of this Dominoes edition of
Emma is available on cassette ISBN 0 19 424359 1

No unauthorized photocopying

Printed in China

The publisher would like to thank the following for permission to reproduce photographs:

The Bridgeman Art Library, London pp 13 (The Circus, Bath by Thomas Malton Jnr, courtesy of the Victoria Art
Gallery, Bath and North East Somerset Council), 25 (evening dresses for August 1808 from 'Le Beau Monde'
courtesy of the Trustees of the V&A); Ronald Grant Archive pp 56 (Wuthering Heights, Much Ado About
Nothing), 58 (James Dean, Marilyn Monroe, Cleopatra); The Press Association p 58 (Britney Spears/Fiona
Hanson); Rex Features, London p 58 (Ricky Martin, Prince William, Ayrton Senna, Naomi Campbell); Courtesy of
the Trustees of the V&A p 7 (detail from She Stoops to Conquer by Francis Wheatley p15-1947).

Dominoes

SERIES EDITORS: BILL BOWLER AND SUE PARMINTER

Emma

JANE AUSTEN

Text adaptation by Barbara Mackay

Illustrated by Susan Scott

LEVEL TWO ■ 700 HEADWORDS

Jane Austen (1775–1817) spent most of her life in Hampshire, in the south of England. Her life was quiet, and she never married, although she lived happily with her family and friends. Her novels, including *Emma, Sense and Sensibility*, and *Pride and Prejudice*, are some of the greatest novels in English. They have been adapted for film and television many times.

OXFORD

BEFORE READING

Here are some of the people in the story *Emma*.

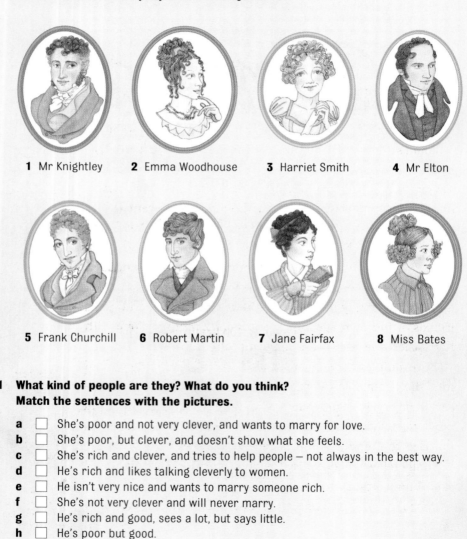

1 Mr Knightley **2** Emma Woodhouse **3** Harriet Smith **4** Mr Elton

5 Frank Churchill **6** Robert Martin **7** Jane Fairfax **8** Miss Bates

1 **What kind of people are they? What do you think?**
Match the sentences with the pictures.

a ☐ She's poor and not very clever, and wants to marry for love.
b ☐ She's poor, but clever, and doesn't show what she feels.
c ☐ She's rich and clever, and tries to help people – not always in the best way.
d ☐ He's rich and likes talking cleverly to women.
e ☐ He isn't very nice and wants to marry someone rich.
f ☐ She's not very clever and will never marry.
g ☐ He's rich and good, sees a lot, but says little.
h ☐ He's poor but good.

2 **What do you think happens between these people in the book?**
Who falls in love with whom?

CHAPTER 1

Emma is interested in Harriet

Emma Woodhouse had everything. She was beautiful, clever and rich, and she lived very comfortably with her father in a fine house called Hartfield in the village of Highbury.

Emma's life as a young child **became** unhappy when her mother died, so Mr Woodhouse found a woman called Miss Taylor to teach Emma and her sister Isabella. Later, when Emma's sister married Mr John Knightley and went to live in London, Miss Taylor soon became more of a friend than a **governess** to Emma.

After Miss Taylor married and moved away, Emma **missed** her friend and her good conversation greatly. Emma and her father knew many people in Highbury, but she had no good friends of her own age. She spent many evenings alone with her father and they were long and often boring.

One evening after supper, an old friend of the family walked into the room. Mr George Knightley was a man of thirty-seven or thirty-eight years who lived near Highbury and often visited Emma and her father. His brother John was married to Emma's sister, Isabella.

'Shall I tell you about Miss Taylor's **wedding**, Mr Knightley?' said Emma, trying to sound happy.

'Poor Emma,' said her father. 'She misses Miss Taylor very much.'

'Of course Emma misses her friend,' said Mr Knightley, 'but I'm sure she is happy that Miss Taylor has married.'

'Yes, I am,' said Emma smiling. 'And don't forget that they

become (*past* **became**) to begin to be

governess a woman who lives with and teaches children in their home

miss to want something that you once had, but that you don't have now

wedding the day when two people marry

married because of me. I decided it four years ago when you
all said that Mr Weston didn't want to marry again.'

'Oh, dear,' said Mr Woodhouse. 'Please don't **matchmake**
any more, Emma. Things always happen as you say they will.'

'But, Papa, I *love* matchmaking,' replied Emma, laughing.

'Mr Weston married Miss Taylor because he loves her and
she loves him, not because he met her through you,' said
Mr Knightley, shaking his head.

'But, Mr Knightley,' she said. 'I knew how they felt before

they knew it themselves. That is the secret of a good matchmaker!'

Emma sometimes asked a group of her father's friends to spend the evening at Hartfield. On one of these evenings Emma felt very excited. A young woman of seventeen was coming to the party. She had no friends or family but she was very beautiful. Her name was Harriet Smith.

Emma was interested in Harriet and they spent the evening talking. Harriet was not very clever, but she was friendly, kind, and had beautiful blue eyes. When Harriet and her father's friends left, Emma made a plan. She wanted to teach Harriet, to be her friend, and to **introduce** her to the important people in Highbury.

Emma started to spend a lot of time with Harriet and she soon knew all about her. Harriet told her about her friends, the Martins. She often stayed with them on their **farm**, and she liked Mr Robert Martin very much.

One day while the young women were out walking, they met Mr Martin. Emma saw at once that Harriet liked him a lot, and she was very unhappy about it. A farmer was not the right husband for beautiful Harriet! Emma decided to be Harriet's matchmaker.

Emma soon thought of the right person for Harriet. It was Mr Elton – a **handsome** young **clergyman** with a comfortable home who needed a wife. Emma started work at once. She spoke to Harriet about Mr Elton and to Mr Elton about Harriet, and planned lots of ways for them to meet.

Mr Elton started to visit Hartfield often, and Emma was sure that her plan was working well.

'I see that you have taught Miss Smith a lot and have helped her to become a much better person,' Mr Elton told Emma one day.

introduce to bring people together for the first time by saying their names and something about them

farm a place in the country where people keep cows, sheep and other animals

handsome good-looking (a man is handsome but a woman is beautiful)

clergyman a man who works for the church

3

'Oh no,' said Emma smiling. 'Harriet has always been kind and beautiful. I have done very little.'

'You are always right, Emma,' replied Mr Elton warmly. Emma was sure that he spoke with love in his eyes, and at once, she thought of a new plan.

'Would you like me to **paint** your picture Harriet?' Emma asked one day, in front of Mr Elton.

Harriet was unsure, but Mr Elton thought that it was a wonderful plan. Emma began at once. She was a good painter and soon finished a fine picture.

'Do you think that it is a nice picture, Mr Elton?' asked Emma, smiling.

'It is the best picture I have ever seen. It is quite beautiful. You are a very clever painter Emma,' said Mr Elton. 'I shall take it to London for a **frame** at once.'

'He is very handsome and just right for Harriet,' Emma thought to herself, 'but I find him boring.'

While Mr Elton was in London, Harriet arrived at Hartfield one morning with a big surprise.

'Emma, you will never **believe** it,' she said excitedly. 'Mr Martin has asked me to marry him!'

Emma was not happy when she saw that Harriet wanted to say yes to Mr Martin.

'You cannot marry him, Harriet,' she said coldly. 'He is only a farmer. If you marry him, we could not be friends. I could not visit a farmer's wife!'

Poor Harriet! She did what Emma told her and wrote to Mr Martin to say no, but she was very unhappy.

Another person was also unhappy when he heard the news. Mr Knightley knew Mr Martin well and liked him a lot. He was very angry when Emma told him Harriet's answer.

'Did you tell Harriet not to marry him, Emma?' he asked.

'Yes, I did,' replied Emma, smiling sweetly.

'But Mr Martin is a kind, intelligent man. He has a fine

paint to put different colours on paper to make a picture

frame the square piece of wood outside a picture

believe to think that something is true

'It is the best picture I have ever seen.'

home and farm, and Harriet was lucky that he liked her. Harriet has no family and she couldn't find a better husband! You have been no friend to Harriet, Emma,' he said crossly.

Emma did not like Mr Knightley to be angry with her, but she was sure that she was right.

'You are wrong, Mr Knightley,' she said. 'Harriet can marry someone much better than Mr Martin.'

Mr Knightley got up quickly and walked to the door.

'Good morning to you,' he said coldly, and left.

READING CHECK

Are these sentences true or false? Tick the boxes.

		True	False
a	Emma lives alone with her mother.	☐	☑
b	Mr Knightley thinks Emma is good at finding husbands for her friends.	☐	☐
c	Emma decides to help Harriet Smith find a husband.	☐	☐
d	Emma chooses Mr Elton as a good man for Harriet to marry.	☐	☐
e	The farmer Robert Martin wants to marry Harriet.	☐	☐
f	Harriet doesn't like Mr Martin.	☐	☐
g	Mr Knightley thinks Mr Martin could be a good husband for Harriet.	☐	☐
h	Emma listens to Mr Knightley and decides that he is right.	☐	☐

WORD WORK

1 These words don't match the pictures. Correct them.

a ~~to introduce~~ clergyman **b** wedding .... **c** to paint ....

d clergyman ....   **e** farm ....   **f** frame ....

2 **Complete the words to make sentences about the story. All of the words come from Chapter 1.**

a Emma likes to m a t c h m a k e.

b Mr Elton isn't ugly, he's a very h _ _ d _ _ m _ man.

c Emma b _ l _ _ v _ _ that she is always right.

d Miss Taylor came to Hartfield as Emma's g _ v _ _ n _ _ s but she left as Emma's friend.

e Emma m _ _ _ _ s her old friend now she has left Hartfield.

f Mr Knightley b _ c _ _ _ s angry with Emma when she stops Harriet saying yes to marrying Robert Martin.

GUESS WHAT

What happens in the next chapter? Tick three boxes.

a ☐ Emma says she doesn't need a husband.

b ☐ Mr Elton tells Harriet that he wants to marry her.

c ☐ Mr Knightley tells Harriet that he wants to marry her.

d ☐ Mr Elton tells Emma that he wants to marry her.

e ☐ Mr Knightley tells Emma that he wants to marry her.

f ☐ Emma is cold with Mr Knightley.

CHAPTER 2

Emma feels uncomfortable

poem a short piece of careful writing; it is often about what you feel

clear easy to understand

When Mr Elton came back from London with the picture in its frame, he put it in the sitting room at Hartfield and looked at it lovingly. Emma watched him and thought of a new plan.

She and Harriet were making a book of love **poems**, so she asked Mr Elton to write something for it. He happily agreed, and when he finished, he gave his poem to Emma and left the room. It was called *To Miss ____? Emma read the poem to herself quickly.

'Oh Harriet,' she said excitedly. 'It is **clear** that he has written it for you and that he loves you. I'm sure that he will ask you to marry him soon. I'm so happy. I know that I was right to matchmake for you and Mr Elton. Now you must read his poem.'

Emma read the poem to herself quickly.

At first, Harriet could not believe that Mr Elton loved her, but Emma soon **persuaded** her that it was true. Harriet was very happy, and she even stopped thinking about Mr Martin. The next day, she and Emma went for a walk past Mr Elton's house.

'Just think Harriet, one day you will live there as Mrs Elton, a clergyman's wife!' said Emma.

Harriet smiled, and then she looked thoughtful. 'But Emma, what about you? I can't understand why you don't want a husband too,' she said.

'Harriet, I don't *need* a husband!' replied Emma with a **confident** smile.

Emma's sister Isabella and her family came to stay at Hartfield for Christmas. During their visit, Mr and Mrs Weston **invited** them all to their house for dinner. Knowing that Mr Elton was also a **guest**, Emma asked Mrs Weston to invite Harriet too, but in the end Harriet had a cold and could not go.

While they were waiting to leave for the Westons' house, Isabella's husband, Mr John Knightley, turned to Emma. 'I have watched Mr Elton, Emma, and he likes you very, very much,' he said, with a knowing look. 'Do you like him, too?'

Emma laughed. 'We are good friends, that's all. Surely you don't really think that he loves me?' she replied.

At dinner, Mr Elton came and sat next to Emma. He smiled a lot and was very **attentive** to her all evening. Emma remembered John Knightley's words and she felt uncomfortable.

'Mr Elton hasn't spoken about Harriet once this evening,' thought Emma. 'And he is spending all his time with me. If he loves Harriet, that isn't right!'

While she was thinking, Mr Weston spoke to her.

'Emma, we have some news. We have had a letter from my son Frank, and he is coming to visit us,' he said excitedly.

persuade to make somebody change their way of thinking

confident sure of yourself

invite to ask someone to come to your home, or to a party

guest somebody that you invite to your home, or to a party

attentive watching and listening carefully and with interest

9

carriage a kind of car wih horses; rich people travelled in them

'That's wonderful Mr Weston,' said Emma, smiling.

Emma thought that Frank Churchill sounded very interesting and she wanted to meet him. Mr Weston's first wife died when his son Frank was a young child, and the young man now lived with his rich aunt and uncle – Mr and Mrs Churchill. They had no children themselves and Frank was like a son to them. He even changed his name to Churchill to please them.

When it was time to go home, Emma said goodbye, and waited for her **carriage**. To her surprise Mr Elton climbed into it with her. Before she could say anything, he took her hand, looked into her eyes, and told her that he loved her! Emma was so surprised that she did not know what to say.

Neither Emma nor Mr Elton said a word.

'But . . . but . . . Mr Elton,' she cried. 'You can't love me, you love Harriet!'

'Harriet!' cried Mr Elton. 'What are you saying? I've never loved Harriet in my life!' And he thought to himself, 'It's true that Harriet is beautiful, but she isn't rich!'

'No, Emma my dearest,' he went on, 'it is *you* that I love and I thought that you felt the same about me. Say that you will marry me!' he

said, looking deeply into her eyes.

Emma could not believe what was happening. This was not what she planned!

'Mr Elton, please stop this at once!' she cried angrily. 'I will not marry you!'

They both sat there, feeling angry, and neither Emma nor Mr Elton spoke for the rest of the journey.

The next day, Mr Elton left hurriedly for the city of Bath, in the south-west of England. Emma was **relieved** that she did not have to see him for a while.

'I know that Mr Elton doesn't love me! He only wants to marry me for my money,' thought Emma. Then she remembered Harriet! 'Oh dear, and I persuaded Harriet that Mr Elton loved her. Now I will have to tell her!'

Harriet cried a lot when she heard the news, but she did not **blame** Emma, and she did not blame Mr Elton. Because Harriet was so nice about it all, Emma felt worse.

Not long after this, Emma had more bad news. Frank Churchill couldn't come to Highbury until later in the year.

'Oh dear, and I really wanted to meet him. He sounds so interesting,' she said to Mr Knightley who was visiting Hartfield.

'Well I'm sure that he could come if he really wanted to,' replied Mr Knightley coldly. 'I think that he is making an **excuse**.'

Emma was surprised.

'Mr Knightley, why do you say that?' she asked.

'It's clear that his father wants to see him now, not later,' replied Mr Knightley crossly. 'I think that he is a **selfish** young man!'

'Well, I don't,' replied Emma coldly. 'And I'm sure that he will come to Highbury as soon as he can.'

Mr Knightley said nothing after that.

relieved happy that something isn't a problem any more

blame to say that someone did something wrong

excuse something – often untrue – that you say to explain why you can't do something

selfish a person who thinks only of himself or herself

READING CHECK

Put these sentences in the correct order. Number them 1-9.

a ☐ Mr Weston tells Emma that his son, Frank, is coming to Highbury soon.

b ☐ Mr Elton brings Emma's picture of Harriet back from London.

c ☐ Emma is sad that Frank Churchill can't come to Highbury for the moment.

d ☐ Mr Elton writes a love poem and gives it to Emma and Harriet to read.

e ☐ Mr Elton goes away to Bath.

f ☐ Emma and Harriet walk past Mr Elton's house and talk of Harriet living there.

g ☐ Isabella and Mr John Knightley come to Highbury for Christmas.

h ☐ Mr Elton asks Emma to marry him and she says no.

i ☐ Mr John Knightley tells Emma to be careful of Mr Elton.

WORD WORK

Find words in the picture of the carriage to complete the sentences.

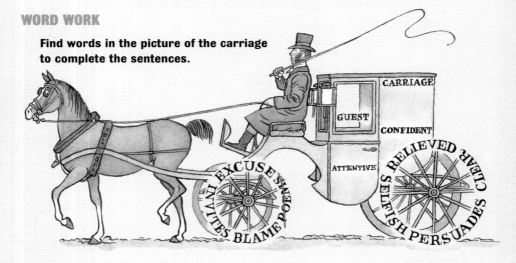

a Byron wrote many p o e m s .

b It's very _ _ _ _ _ from her mistake with Mr Elton that Emma isn't always right about things.

c Mr Knightley is often a _ _ _ _ _ at Emma's house.

d Harriet is very nice and doesn't _ _ _ _ _ Emma when things go wrong.

e You never think of other people. You're very _ _ _ _ _ _ _ _.

f Emma often _ _ _ _ _ _ _ her friends to dinner at Hartfield.

g People often don't say truly why they don't want to do something, they make an _ _ _ _ _ _ _.

h People in Jane Austen's books often travel by _ _ _ _ _ _ _ _ _.

i After her terrible mistake Emma feels _ _ _ _ _ _ _ _ when Mr Elton leaves Highbury for a time.

j Harriet doesn't want to marry Mr Elton, but Emma _ _ _ _ _ _ _ _ _ her that it is a good plan.

k Mr Elton is very _ _ _ _ _ _ _ _ _ to Emma when they have dinner at the Westons' house.

l Emma is a very _ _ _ _ _ _ _ _ _ _ woman. She is very sure of herself.

GUESS WHAT

What happens in the next chapter?

	Yes	Perhaps	No
a Emma visits some people who live in Highbury.	☐	☐	☐
b Harriet goes to Bath to find Mr Elton.	☐	☐	☐
c Mr Elton decides to marry a rich woman from Bristol.	☐	☐	☐
d Frank Churchill comes to Highbury.	☐	☐	☐
e Frank falls in love with Harriet.	☐	☐	☐
f Frank and Emma spend some time together.	☐	☐	☐
g Mr Knightley likes hearing about Frank.	☐	☐	☐

CHAPTER 3

Emma doesn't like Jane

A few days later, while Emma and Harriet were out walking, they decided to visit Mrs and Miss Bates. Mrs Bates was a **widow** who lived in Highbury with her unmarried daughter. Miss Bates was a kind woman, but she was very **talkative**, and Emma thought she was **silly** and boring. She did not often visit her, but she wanted to introduce her to Harriet.

When Miss Bates saw Emma and Harriet, she was very happy because she had some news to tell them.

'Miss Woodhouse, can you believe what has happened? We have had a letter today from my **niece**, Jane Fairfax, who is living in Weymouth – a very nice town by the sea in the south-west of England. She is coming to stay with us and we are very excited. You like Jane, don't you, Miss Woodhouse? She is a beautiful girl and so clever!'

'Yes, of course, Miss Bates. When is she coming?' replied Emma, trying to sound interested.

'Next week! She is coming for three months and there is so much to do before she arrives,' worried Miss Bates.

'Then, after her time with us, Jane will look for a job as a governess,' said Mrs Bates unhappily.

Jane Fairfax was the same age as Emma, but they were not good friends. It was true that Jane was beautiful and clever. Everybody who knew her liked her, but Emma was a little **jealous** of Jane. She liked being the *only* beautiful and clever young woman in Highbury.

Like Harriet, Jane Fairfax did not have any family or money, and without a rich husband she needed to work. Emma did not like Jane, but she felt sorry for her. So when she saw her again, she tried to be friendly.

widow a woman whose husband is dead

talkative talking a lot

silly stupid

niece your sister's (or brother's) daughter

jealous feeling angry or sad because you want to be like somebody else

Jane was not very talkative.

'I believe you met Frank Churchill while you were in Weymouth, Jane,' said Emma cheerfully.

'Yes, I did,' replied Jane.

'He is coming to visit Mr and Mrs Weston in Highbury soon,' said Emma, trying to smile. 'Did you know?'

'Oh, really,' replied Jane, looking uninterested.

'I think that he sounds a very nice man. Did you like him?' Emma asked.

'People say that he is a very nice man. I do not really know him myself,' replied Jane coldly.

Jane was not very talkative and Emma found the conversation difficult. 'What is the matter with her?' she thought crossly. 'Why is she being so cold and so unfriendly?'

After that difficult afternoon, Emma did not really want to see Jane again very soon, but the next day Miss Bates and Jane came to visit her at Hartfield.

'Emma, have you heard?' said Miss Bates, excitedly. 'Mr Elton is going to marry someone called Miss Hawkins from Bristol. I hear that she is very beautiful and very rich!'

Emma could not believe this news! Could Mr Elton have forgotten his words of love to her so soon?

'But he has only been away for four weeks!' she said.

'Yes, I know! He's a lucky man. And after the wedding he will bring his **bride** back to Highbury. Isn't that good news?' said Miss Bates smiling happily.

Emma did *not* think that it was very good news!

'So, I was right about Mr Elton,' thought Emma to herself. 'He was just looking for a rich wife and that's why he asked me and not Harriet to marry him.'

Mr Elton came back to Highbury for a short visit before the wedding. Poor Harriet did not want to see him, but luckily she and Emma soon heard some news which stopped them thinking about Mr Elton.

'Emma, we have had a letter from Frank,' said Mr Weston. 'He is coming to Highbury tomorrow. I know that you would like to meet him, so I shall bring him to visit you.'

Frank was tall, handsome and friendly, and Emma liked him at once. After tea they agreed to meet the next day, and he left to go and visit Jane Fairfax and Miss Bates.

The next day Emma and Mrs Weston showed Frank around Highbury. They stopped at the Crown **Inn**.

'This is a good place for a party, Emma,' said Frank excitedly. 'Why don't we have a **ball** here?'

'Oh I love dancing. That's a wonderful idea!' cried Emma. 'We can invite Harriet and Mr Knightley, and Jane Fairfax, of course. Did you see her yesterday?'

'Yes, I did, and I met her aunt, Miss Bates,' replied Frank, laughing.

'Did you often see Jane in Weymouth?' asked Emma.

bride a woman on the day of her wedding or soon after it

inn an old word for a hotel where you can eat, drink, or stay

ball a formal party with dancing

'No, not often,' replied Frank. 'And you, are you good friends with her?' he asked.

'I have known her since we were children, but we are not good friends. I think that Jane is too unfriendly to make friends easily,' replied Emma, and Frank quickly agreed with her.

The next day, Emma talked about Frank to her friends.

'He is very handsome, isn't he, Mrs Weston?' she said.

'Oh yes,' replied Mrs Weston. 'Very handsome.'

'And so funny too!' said Emma, smiling to herself.

While they talked, Mr Knightley sat reading his newspaper. He was tired of hearing everyone speak so warmly about Frank Churchill.

READING CHECK

Match the first and second parts of these sentences.

a	Miss Bates is excited . . .	**1**	arrives in Highbury at last.
b	Jane Fairfax is beautiful and clever . . .	**2**	spend a lot of time together.
c	Emma thinks Jane is . . .	**3**	a rich woman from Bristol.
d	Mr Elton plans to marry . . .	**4**	because Jane Fairfax is coming to visit her.
e	Emma realizes that Mr Elton . . .	**5**	doesn't like Frank Churchill.
f	Frank Churchill . . .	**6**	very cold and unfriendly when they meet.
g	Frank and Emma . . .	**7**	was only interested in her money.
h	Mr Knightley . . .	**8**	like Emma, but poor like Harriet.

WORD WORK

Correct the mistakes in these sentences. All the words come from Chapter 3.

a I'd like to stay at an old village **ink**. ......*inn*.......

b Mrs Rose is a **window**; her husband died last year. ....

c She's very **zealous** of her husband. She doesn't like him to talk to

other women. ....

d In Oxford and Cambridge many students go to **falls** in June. ....

e I have one **piece** – my sister's daughter. Her name's Miranda. ....

f Don't be **silky**! Moscow isn't in Poland! ....

g After they married, he took his **pride** home to meet his parents. ....

h She's a very **walkative** person – she never stops speaking. ....

GUESS WHAT

What happens in the next chapter? Tick the boxes.

a   gets a present from someone.

☐ Emma   ☐ Jane Fairfax

b Someone tells
Emma that   is in love with Jane.

☐ Mr Knightley   ☐ Frank Churchill

c   sing together at a party.

☐ Emma and Frank   ☐ Jane and Frank

 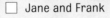

d Mr Knightley doesn't
want to visit Miss Bates's
house when   is a guest there.

☐ Robert Martin   ☐ Frank Churchill

CHAPTER 4

Is someone secretly in love?

Some time later, Mr and Mrs Cole, who lived in Highbury, decided to have a dinner party.

While they were waiting for all the guests to arrive, Frank Churchill came and sat next to Emma, and they talked. In the middle of their conversation Emma **overheard** Mrs Cole say something very interesting.

'Did you know that Jane Fairfax has a **piano** now? It arrived today and nobody knows who sent it!' said Mrs Cole excitedly to her **neighbour**.

'A piano!' thought Emma. 'That's a very expensive present. I **wonder** who sent it?'

Frank saw her looking thoughtful. 'Maybe Jane Fairfax has an **admirer**,' he said playfully, and smiled at her.

'Don't be silly,' said Emma, laughing. 'I believe that **Colonel** Campbell sent it. He looked after her when she was a child, and is like a father to her. I'm sure that he sent it. I really don't think that Jane has an admirer,' she went on, 'or that she is looking for a husband. She is too unfriendly for that.'

'Yes, I'm sure that you're right,' agreed Frank immediately.

Later that evening, Mrs Weston came and sat next to Emma, and they talked about Jane Fairfax's piano.

'You know, *I* think that Mr George Knightley sent it,' said Mrs Weston.

'Mr Knightley!' said Emma, in surprise.

'Yes. I think that Mr Knightley is Jane's secret admirer,' replied Mrs Weston, talking quietly. 'You know that he loves listening to Jane play the piano. He always says that she has the best voice he has ever heard. And this evening he sent his carriage for her and Miss Bates to travel in.'

overhear (*past* **overheard**) to listen secretly to someone talking

piano a big musical instrument that you play by pressing black and white keys

neighbour a person sitting next to someone

wonder to want to know something

admirer an old word for a person who likes or loves another person, often secretly

colonel an important soldier in the army

'But that isn't anything unusual,' said Emma. 'Mr Knightley knows that they don't have a carriage and he is always very kind to Miss Bates.'

'Well, *I* think that he sent it because he is secretly in love with Jane,' said Mrs Weston, smiling in a playful way.

'No, no, Mrs Weston, I am sure that you are wrong. I know Mr Knightley better than anyone,' said Emma confidently. 'Jane and he are too different. Mr Knightley is so warm and kind and Jane Fairfax is so cold! No, it isn't possible. And don't forget, Mrs Weston,' said Emma. 'Mr Knightley is like me. He doesn't want to marry.'

But Emma could not persuade Mrs Weston to believe her.

Just then, everyone decided that it was time for some music. First Emma played the piano and she and Frank sang some songs together. Everyone agreed that they were a very handsome **couple**. After a few songs, Emma went back to her seat and Jane sat at the piano and played and sang with Frank. She played the piano really beautifully and she had a better voice than Emma too.

Emma looked at Mr Knightley, who was watching Jane and smiling. It was clear that he loved listening to her.

Emma looked at Mr Knightley.

glare to look angrily at somebody

whisper to speak very quietly

Everyone wanted Jane to sing song after song, but she was becoming tired. When Frank asked her to sing another song, Mr Knightley **glared** at him and **whispered** to Miss Bates, 'Miss Bates, please tell Jane to stop. She is too tired and if she sings another song she will be ill.'

Emma was surprised. 'He *is* being attentive to Jane. I wonder if Mrs Weston is right?' she thought to herself.

After the music, everyone wanted to dance. Emma loved dancing, and Frank was the first to ask her. As she danced, she looked around to see what Mr Knightley and Jane were doing. She was happy to see that Jane was already dancing, and that Mr Knightley was talking to Mrs Cole.

She got up at once and went to the window.

22

Frank was a fine dancer, and Emma soon forgot about Mr Knightley possibly being Jane Fairfax's secret admirer.

The next morning, Emma thought about the party and smiled. She was a little unhappy that she could not play the piano or sing as well as Jane, but she did not worry too much about it. Emma knew that she really needed to **practise** more, but she also knew that she was too **lazy** to do it!

The next day, she met Harriet, and they went shopping in Highbury. In town they saw Mrs Weston and Frank.

'We're going to visit Miss Bates and to listen to Jane playing her new piano. Please say that you will come too,' said Frank, smiling at Emma.

Emma didn't really want to listen to Jane playing the piano again, but she decided that she wanted to spend some more time together with Frank. So they all went to Miss Bates's house together. Soon after they arrived, while they were listening to Jane playing, Miss Bates saw Mr Knightley riding his horse past the house. She got up at once and went to the window.

'Mr Knightley,' she called. 'Thank you for sending your carriage for us last night. Miss Woodhouse and Miss Smith are here. We are all listening to Jane playing the piano. Come in and have some tea with us.'

'Perhaps I will. But how is Jane? Is she well?' Mr Knightley called back. 'I hope that all her singing last night didn't hurt her voice.'

'No, no, she is quite well, thank you,' replied Miss Bates. 'Will you come in for some tea now, Mr Knightley? Mrs Weston and Frank Churchill are here also.'

'Oh dear. I'm afraid I don't have time today, Miss Bates, but thank you. Perhaps some other time. Goodbye to you,' said Mr Knightley, and he rode away.

practise to do something again and again so that you become better at it

lazy not wanting to work

activities

READING CHECK

Correct eight more mistakes in the chapter summary.

dinner

Mr and Mrs Cole have a ~~lunch~~ party. Emma goes to it and sits next to Mr Knightley. Emma

learns that Jane has a new guitar. Mrs Weston thinks Mr Knightley is in love with Miss

Bates. Emma and Frank write some songs together. Then Jane sings and plays some

songs. Mr Knightley listens to her happily, but he doesn't want her to sing too long and

hurt her eyes. After that Jane and Frank Churchill dance together.

The next day Emma goes shopping with Harriet in Highbury. They meet Mrs Cole and Frank

there. Together they all go to Miss Bates' house to hear Jane play some more music.

Mr Knightley rides past on a bicycle but he doesn't want to come in.

WORD WORK

Match the words in the piano with the underlined words.

a Mr Knightley <u>looks angrily</u> at Frank. ....glares....

b Emma <u>wants to know</u> where Jane's piano comes from. ....

c Mr Knightley sees Jane is tired and he <u>speaks very quietly</u> to Miss Bates to tell Jane to stop singing. ....

d Emma doesn't <u>play pieces again and again</u> on the piano very much. ....

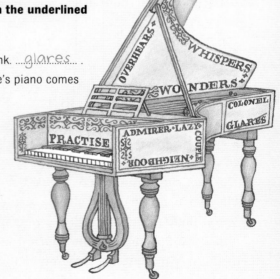

OVERHEARS WHISPERS WONDERS COLONEL GLARES ADMIRER LAZY COUPLE NEIGHBOUR PRACTISE

24

e Mrs Weston thinks Jane has got a secret <u>lover</u>. ....

f Mr and Mrs Cole are a nice <u>man and woman</u>. ....

g Emma <u>listens secretly to</u> Mrs Cole speaking about Jane's new piano. ....

h When it comes to practising the piano, Emma is really <u>not interested in working hard</u>. ....

i That's the <u>important soldier</u> over there! ....

j Mrs Cole said something to the <u>woman sitting next to her</u> on her left. ....

GUESS WHAT

What happens in the next chapter? Tick the boxes.

1 Emma . . .
  a ☐ doesn't spend any time with Frank.
  b ☐ decides that she isn't in love with Frank.
  c ☐ worries that Frank is perhaps in love with her.

2 Harriet . . .
  a ☐ decides that Emma is not her friend.
  b ☐ doesn't want to meet Mr Elton again.
  c ☐ gets a cold.

3 Jane . . .
  a ☐ becomes Mrs Elton's friend.
  b ☐ is very happy with her life.
  c ☐ doesn't want to find a job.

4 Mr Knightley . . .
  a ☐ wants to marry Harriet.
  b ☐ doesn't speak to Emma.
  c ☐ thinks Jane is nice.

CHAPTER 5

The Eltons arrive in Highbury

organize to get
something ready

Everyone enjoyed dancing at Mr and Mrs Coles's house, so Frank and Emma decided that they really had to begin **organizing** the ball at the Inn in the village. Mr Weston happily agreed to pay the cost of using a large room at the Crown for the evening.

'Emma, will you promise to have the first two dances at the Crown with me?' Frank asked her hopefully.

'Yes, of course,' replied Emma. She was pleased that Frank wanted to dance with her first.

They were soon busy getting things ready.

*Emma told
Mr Knightley
of their plans
for the ball.*

When Emma told Mr Knightley of their plans for the ball, he was not very nice about it.

'If Mr Weston wants to pay a lot of money to the Crown, and you want to have the trouble of getting everything ready for weeks, and all for one evening of noisy dancing, eating and drinking, I won't stop you,' he said. 'I will go to the ball of course, to please you, and I will try not to fall asleep. But I won't enjoy myself, I'm sure.'

Was Mr Knightley uninterested in the ball because he didn't ever dance himself; or was he perhaps angry, because Emma didn't talk to him about her plans before she began to get things ready with Frank? She found it difficult to say.

'But Mr Knightley, what about watching everyone dancing? You would like that, surely?' Emma went on.

'No, Emma,' answered Mr Knightley. 'I would not. I prefer staying at home to going out to balls.'

Emma talked to Jane Fairfax about the plans for the ball; and she was very interested in what Jane had to say.

'A ball! How wonderful! I love going to balls! I hope nothing will stop this one.'

Emma thought back to Mrs Weston's words about Mr Knightley being in love with Jane. 'Now I'm sure that story isn't true,' she said to herself. 'Because Mr Knightley really doesn't want to go to the ball, and Miss Fairfax really does want to.'

But before they could have the ball at the Crown, Frank got some bad news. His **mother** was ill and he had to go back to London to see her.

'Oh Frank, I'm so sorry!' said Emma unhappily. 'We'll have to **postpone** the ball. We can't have it without you!'

'I'm sorry too, Emma,' said Frank. 'But I'll come back as soon as I can. I'll miss you all very much.'

Emma was very unhappy and thought about Frank all the time during the first few days that he was away.

'I miss Frank a lot,' she thought, looking out of her bedroom window one night. 'I wonder if I'm in love with him?'

mother Frank calls his aunt, Mrs Churchill, this

postpone to do something at a later time

embarrassed
feeling shy or worried about what other people think of you

Then one day Emma heard some news which made her forget about Frank for a little while. Mr Elton and his bride were travelling back to Highbury. Emma knew that Harriet was very worried about seeing Mr Elton again, and she felt sorry for her.

'Harriet, don't worry. Mr Elton has a wife now and I'm sure that he has forgotten about our silly mistake,' said Emma.

'But Emma, I'm so **embarrassed**. I hope he doesn't speak to me. I won't know where to look!' replied poor Harriet.

As soon as the Eltons arrived in Highbury, Mr Elton took his wife to meet the people of the village. One day they came to Hartfield.

Mrs Elton was a loud woman who loved talking, mostly about herself and her family. She talked a lot about her brother's house and how it was very like Hartfield, but larger and better!

'What a rude woman!' thought Emma.

'What a **rude** woman!' thought Emma angrily. 'I really don't like her, and I'm sure that Frank won't like her either.'

Mrs Elton did not really like Emma. It was clear from the way she spoke that she knew all about Harriet **foolishly** believing Mr Elton was in love with her, and about Emma's part in the story, but she was looking for a friend in Highbury and so she tried to be nice. But Emma was **quite** cold with her. In the end, Mrs Elton left Hartfield feeling **disappointed**. She decided that she would try to become Jane Fairfax's friend **instead of** Emma Woodhouse's.

'Poor Jane!' said Emma to her friends after this. 'Now she will have to listen to Mrs Elton all the time!'

'Jane is beautiful and clever, Emma. It is no surprise that Mrs Elton wants her for a friend,' replied Mr Knightley quietly.

'We all know that you like Jane, Mr Knightley. Perhaps more than you would like to say openly?' said Emma, turning to Mrs Weston.

Mr Knightley looked embarrassed. 'Emma, are you matchmaking again?' he asked.

'Oh no, Mr Knightley. I have learnt my lesson. I am just saying what some people are thinking,' she replied.

Mr Knightley looked thoughtful and then he got up to leave.

'Well Emma, it is true that I **admire** Jane, but if you think that I am in love with her, then I'm afraid you are wrong,' he said calmly, and left.

'Well, Mrs Weston, what do you say to that?' asked Emma.

'I say,' said Mrs Weston smiling, 'that Mr Knightley was embarrassed because you spoke the **truth**!'

Emma really did not like Mrs Elton, but she felt that she had to arrange a small dinner party for her. Harriet was very relieved that she was busy that night and could not go.

The party went well. But at one moment in the evening

rude not polite

foolishly stupidly

quite a little

disappointed unhappy when you don't get what you want

instead of in the place of

admire to think that somebody (or something) is very good

truth when what you say is true

Mrs Elton turned to Jane and said, 'Now Jane, what are you going to do? It is April now and you still haven't found a job as a governess yet! I think that I will have to help you. I will write to my friend Mrs Bragge and perhaps you can go and work for her,' she said.

'Thank you, Mrs Elton,' said Jane quietly, 'but I'm not looking for a job yet. Colonel and Mrs Campbell are coming home soon and I want to spend some time with them first.'

'Don't be silly Jane. It is more important that you find yourself a job. I'm sure that the Campbells will agree with me about that,' replied Mrs Elton.

'But Mrs Elton—' began Jane.

'Now, don't worry Jane. I will arrange everything,' said Mrs Elton loudly and she turned away.

Poor Jane! She looked very unhappy, and Emma could understand why. It was clearly terrible for her to have Mrs Elton so busy organizing her life all the time. Luckily Mr Weston arrived just then, and the conversation went on to other, happier things.

'Hello, my dear friends,' said Mr Weston, walking into the room with a **cheerful** smile.

'I have just come back from London with news from Frank,' he said. 'His mother is better, so he can come and visit us again. Isn't that wonderful?'

Mrs Weston looked at her husband and they both turned to Emma and smiled.

'Er . . . yes . . . yes, it is,' said Emma thoughtfully.

That evening at home, Emma **realized** something. She wasn't thinking about Frank very much now. She did not even miss him!

cheerful happy

realize to understand something suddenly

'Oh dear. I thought that I loved Frank, but now I realize that I don't!' she thought to herself. 'I like him, of course, but I'm not in love with him. What will I do if *he* loves *me*?'

Emma's worries were unnecessary. When Frank came back

to Highbury again they talked and laughed together for hours, but it was very clear that Frank was really not in love with her.

'Oh, good,' said Emma to herself, feeling relieved. 'I'm sure that Frank and I both feel the same. We aren't in love, but we can still be friends.'

Emma realized something.

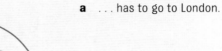
READING CHECK

Match the sentences with the people.

1 Mr Elton

2 Frank

3 Emma

4 Mrs Elton

5 Jane

6 Mr Knightley

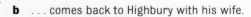

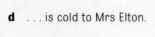

a . . . has to go to London.

b . . . comes back to Highbury with his wife.

c . . . is a loud, talkative woman.

d . . . is cold to Mrs Elton.

e . . . tells Emma that he is not in love with Jane.

f . . . doesn't like Mrs Elton organizing her life.

WORD WORK

Complete the sentences with words from the crossword.

Crossword letters: q / p u d / o r g a n i z e — d i / s t s / t e r a / p e p / f o o l i s h l y a p / n l o / c h e e r f u l i i / u z n / d t e t / e m b a r r a s s e d / u d / t / h

a Emma and Frank begin to
organize a ball at the Crown Inn.

b When Frank leaves for London,
they .... the ball
until he comes back.

c Harriet goes red when Mr Elton
comes back to Highbury; she
feels very ....

d Because she doesn't think of him much when
he's not there, Emma .... that she is not in
love with Frank.

e Mrs Elton doesn't think of how other people feel very much;
she's a very .... woman.

f Harriet isn't very clever; she .... believed what Emma told her about Mr Elton.

g It is better to speak the .... and not say to things which are untrue.

h Mr Weston always has a smile on his face; he's a very .... man.

i Mrs Elton wants Emma to be her friend, and when it is clear that Emma doesn't
like her, she feels ....

j Emma wasn't *very* cold to Mrs Elton, but she was .... cold.

GUESS WHAT

What happens in the next chapter? Match the first and second parts of these sentences.

1	Emma and Harriet go together . . .	**a**	has fun there.
2	Everyone . . .	**b**	with another man.
3	Mr Knightley . . .	**c**	to the ball at the Crown Inn.
4	Harriet falls in love . . .	**d**	is rude to Harriet.
5	Mr Elton . . .	**e**	has a headache after listening to Mrs Elton for hours.
6	Jane . . .	**f**	is friendly with Emma.

CHAPTER 6

A handsome couple

Now that Frank was back, they could finally have the ball at the Crown Inn. When the day arrived, Emma and Harriet travelled there together. This was Harriet's first ball and she was very excited.

When it was time to dance, Frank came up to Emma. 'Emma remember that you promised me the first two dances,' he said playfully.

'Of course,' replied Emma, smiling at him.

While they were dancing, Mr and Mrs Weston watched them. Emma danced beautifully and looked so happy.

'Oh yes, I'm sure that they are in love,' thought Mrs Weston.

While she was dancing, Emma looked around the room and saw Mr Knightley talking to some of the older men. He looked up and smiled at her.

'I know that Mr Knightley doesn't like dancing,' thought Emma, 'but I'm sure that he would be good at it, and he looks so handsome this evening.'

Everyone was having fun, and the evening went quickly. When it was time for the last two dances, Emma of course was dancing with Frank, but Harriet did not have a **partner**.

'Oh, dear,' thought Emma, feeling worried. 'Ah, but I see Mr Elton is there. I'm sure that he will ask Harriet to dance.'

Mr Elton was standing next to Harriet, but he did not ask her to dance. He **ignored** her! Poor Harriet was very embarrassed and she **blushed**. Emma wanted to help, but she couldn't leave Frank alone in the middle of the **dance floor**. Just then she saw Mr Knightley walk across the room and ask Harriet to dance.

'Only Mr Knightley could be so kind,' thought Emma. 'And only Mr Elton could be so rude!'

partner someone to dance with

ignore to decide not to see or speak to someone

blush to become red in the face because you are shy or embarrassed

dance floor the place where people dance at a party or ball

Harriet looked very happy, and while Emma watched them dancing, she **noticed** that Mr Knightley was a surprisingly good dancer! At the end of the dance she decided to go to him and speak to him **privately**.

'You were very kind to help Harriet like that, Mr Knightley,' she said. 'Mr Elton is a very rude and unkind person.'

'Yes. I'm sure that you'll agree that your plans for Mr Elton to marry Harriet were wrong,' said Mr Knightley kindly. 'I think that Harriet had a lucky escape!' and he smiled.

Emma smiled too. 'Yes, I was wrong. I can see that now.'

Just then, Mr Weston came up to them. 'Come on Emma, it's time for the last dance.'

'Who are you going to dance with?' asked Mr Knightley.

Emma turned and smiled at him. 'You, if you will ask me,' she replied. 'Now I know that you can dance!'

Mr Knightley walked across the room and asked Harriet to dance.

notice to see

privately in secret, with no other people near to overhear

35

Emma was happy that she and Mr Knightley were friends again. The next day, while she was thinking about the ball, Frank and Harriet arrived at Hartfield.

'I found Harriet alone on the road to Highbury,' said Frank, looking worried. 'Some **gypsy** children were **chasing** her and she was very **frightened**.'

'Oh Emma, it was terrible,' said Harriet crying. 'But then Frank **rescued** me and chased the gypsies away,' she said, looking at Frank with her beautiful blue eyes.

'What an adventure!' thought Emma, 'And what a handsome couple they are! I didn't think of it before, but perhaps . . .'

A fortnight later Harriet told Emma a secret. 'Emma, I don't think of Mr Elton now. There is another man I think of, but I know that he could never love me,' she said unhappily.

'She is speaking about Frank, of course,' thought Emma excitedly. 'Oh, Harriet,' she said aloud. 'I'm sure that I know who you mean, and I thought that the way he rescued you was wonderful! Perhaps he is the man for you.'

'Oh!' said Harriet. 'Do you really think so?'

'Yes, I do. But we mustn't do anything until we are sure that he feels the same as you,' said Emma. 'This is our secret and we won't talk about it again. We will wait and watch.'

One afternoon, some of Emma's friends were at Hartfield. While they were playing cards, Mr Knightley was watching Frank and he noticed something. He saw that Frank was secretly smiling at Jane, and Jane was looking sweetly at him.

'I thought that Frank was in love with Emma,' thought Mr Knightley. 'Surely he isn't in love with Jane, too!'

'Oh don't be so silly, Mr Knightley,' replied Emma confidently, when he told her. '*I* know who Frank is in love with,' she thought to herself. 'And it *isn't* Jane!'

So Mr Knightley decided to watch Frank closely.

gypsy somebody who doesn't live in a house but travels around the country

chase to run after someone

frightened afraid

rescue to save somebody from danger

Emma went to pick strawberries with the others.

The weather was fine now, so one day Mr Knightley invited everyone to his house, Donwell Abbey, to **pick** the **strawberries** there.

Donwell Abbey was a very fine house and after walking around the beautiful gardens, Emma went to pick strawberries with the others. She saw Mr Knightley and Harriet picking strawberries together, and she heard Mrs Elton talking to Jane on the other side of the strawberry **bed**. She was telling her about a job. Later, when Emma went inside, she found Jane there looking tired.

'I'm going to walk home, Emma. I have a terrible headache, but please don't tell anyone until I have gone.'

Emma agreed not to say anything, and Jane left. A short while later Frank arrived late, hot, tired, and cross.

'I've just seen Jane outside. Why is she going home so early?' he said angrily.

'She has a headache,' replied Emma. 'Now don't be cross Frank. Think about our **picnic** at Box Hill tomorrow. It will be great fun.'

pick to take fruit from a tree or plant

strawberry a small, soft, red fruit

bed a place in a garden for growing fruit or vegetables

picnic a meal that people eat outside in the country, often sitting on the ground

READING CHECK

Choose the correct names to complete the sentences.

a Emma dances the first two dances with . . .
☑ Frank Churchill.
☐ Mr Weston.

b Harriet dances with . . .
☐ Mr Elton.
☐ Mr Knightley.

c
☐ Mr Knightley
☐ Frank Churchill
helps Harriet when some poor children run after her.

d Mr Knightley thinks Frank Churchill is perhaps in love with . . .
☐ Jane Fairfax.
☐ Mrs Elton.

e Emma thinks Frank Churchill could marry . . .
☐ Miss Bates.
☐ Harriet Smith.

WORD WORK

Find the words and complete the sentences.

a In summer lots of people have p <u>i c n i c s</u> in the country or on the beach.

b Dogs often c _ _ _ _ cats.

c Look at that big red apple on the tree! Can I p _ _ _ it?

d S _ _ _ _ _ _ _ _ _ _ _ are my favourite summer fruit.

e Help! Help! Can't someone r _ _ _ _ _ me?

f Emma thinks Frank is a very
good dancing p _ _ _ _ _ _ _.

g Let's not speak about that in front of everyone!
You can tell me p _ _ _ _ _ _ _ _ _ about it later.

h Harriet b _ _ _ _ _ _ when she sees
Mr Elton and he doesn't speak to her.

i Mr Elton doesn't want to speak to Harriet,
so he decides to i _ _ _ _ _ her.

GUESS WHAT

**What happens the next chapter? Write Emma,
Miss Bates, Jane or Mrs Elton in each sentence.**

a .... talks playfully with Frank.

b .... says some silly things.

c .... is rude to Miss Bates.

d .... gets embarrassed because of Emma.

e .... makes Jane take a job as a governess.

f .... becomes ill.

g .... is going to marry Frank.

CHAPTER 7

Emma blushes

The next day was sunny and a fine day for a picnic, but it was a long way to Box Hill, and when they finally arrived, everyone was hot and uncomfortable.

Frank, Emma and Harriet sat down together but Frank was very quiet. Emma was a **vain** girl and she did not like Frank to ignore her. So, forgetting about Harriet for a while, she began to **flirt** with him.

'Come on Frank,' she said smiling playfully. 'Think of something funny that we can do. I'm bored.'

Frank laughed. 'Come on everyone,' he said. 'Emma is bored. Let's think of two clever things to say, a poem or a story perhaps, and three silly things to say. Emma promises to laugh at them all,' and Frank smiled sweetly at her.

Miss Bates turned to him, 'Well, I know that I can't think of two clever things to say but I can always think of three silly things,' she said laughing.

'Ah! Miss Bates,' replied Emma quickly, 'the difficult thing for you will be to say *only* three silly things.'

vain too pleased with how you look and what you can do

flirt to look at someone, smile at them, and talk with them in a playful way because you like them

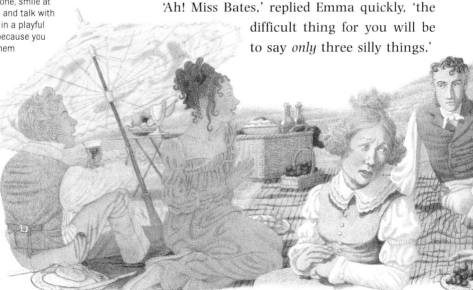

40

'Oh yes, of course,' said Miss Bates looking embarrassed. 'I . . . I . . . I'm always very silly. You're right. I'm sorry, very sorry. I'll be quiet,' and she blushed and turned away.

Nobody thought of poor Miss Bates any more. They were already busy listening to Mr Weston, who was playing the game.

After a few minutes Mrs Elton got up. 'I don't really like this game Emma, so Mr Elton and I are going for a walk.'

A short while later, Jane and Miss Bates got up too, and Mr Knightley followed them. Emma was not enjoying herself now, and she was bored with flirting with Frank. She felt happy when it was finally time to go home. While she was waiting for her carriage, Mr Knightley came up to her.

'Emma, I have to talk to you. And I must speak the

'I'm sorry, very sorry.'

truth because we are friends,' he said. He looked very angry, and then he went on in a cold, hard voice. 'How could you be so rude to Miss Bates?' he asked her. 'Miss Bates is a sweet, kind person. You have everything in the world, and she has nothing. It was very wrong of you to talk to her like that in front of everyone. Why can't you be kinder to people who aren't as lucky as you are?'

Emma knew that Mr Knightley was right, and she felt very **ashamed**. With every word that he spoke she felt worse, and in the end she turned her face away from him to hide her **tears**. She did not want Mr Knightley to see her cry. At last her carriage arrived and, without another word, without looking back, she climbed into it. Mr Knightley could not see her face and he just thought that she was cross with him.

That evening, while Emma sat with her father, she thought about the picnic. She remembered her unkind words to Miss Bates and every word of Mr Knightley's. She was so ashamed of herself that she decided to visit Miss Bates the next day.

'Please come in, Emma,' said Miss Bates kindly. 'Have you come to see Jane? I am afraid she has a bad headache and is in bed. I am so sorry, but she can't see anyone today.'

'Oh, I am sorry Jane is feeling ill,' replied Emma truthfully. 'I hope nothing is the matter.'

'Well, yes there is something. You see Jane is going to leave us. She is going to work as a governess for Mrs Smallridge,' said Miss Bates unhappily. 'Mrs Elton has arranged everything,' she went on. 'At first, Jane said no. She wanted to talk to Colonel and Mrs Campbell first, but Mrs Elton would not listen. Finally, poor Jane said yes, but now she has a bad headache and feels ill.'

Emma knew that Jane did not want to be a governess and that she did not want Mrs Elton's help. She understood **exactly** why Jane felt so ill.

ashamed sorry and unhappy about something you have done

tear the water that comes from your eye when you cry

exactly in all ways

'Oh dear, when does she have to leave?' asked Emma.

'In a fortnight,' replied Miss Bates. 'It's too soon, my dear Emma. My mother and I are very unhappy about it, but . . . oh dear, so much is happening. And now Frank has left too,' she said. 'He had a letter from his father yesterday. His mother is ill again and he left early this morning. And then there's the piano! What shall we do with it? Jane can't take it with her so it will stay here for now, but . . . oh dear . . .'

'Emma, I have come to say goodbye.'

While Miss Bates talked, Emma listened and thought of Jane. She wanted to help her, to be her friend, but now perhaps it was too late.

'Yes, a lot has happened,' thought Emma while she walked home. When she arrived at Hartfield, to her surprise she saw Mr Knightley and Harriet sitting with her father.

'Emma, I have come to say goodbye,' said Mr Knightley, standing up. 'I am going to stay with John and Isabella in London for a few weeks. I don't know when I'll be back.'

He was quiet and he looked very unhappy. Emma was surprised, and she did not know how to answer him.

'And how were Mrs and Miss Bates, Emma?' asked her father kindly. 'Emma has been to visit them this morning, Mr Knightley.'

Emma blushed, and Mr Knightley looked closely at her. He said nothing, but just for a second, she thought that he looked **pleased**.

'I'm sorry Emma, I must go,' he said. 'I'm already late.' And before she could reply he quickly left the room.

'I hope that he has **forgiven** me,' thought Emma, and she nearly felt happy for the first time that day.

In the next few days Emma tried to help Jane. She invited her to Hartfield and she **offered** to take her out in the carriage, but each time Jane said no and stayed at home.

'I think that Jane is making excuses. She doesn't want to see me, but I can't blame her. I have not been a good friend to her,' thought Emma unhappily.

Emma was very surprised.

During this time Emma heard some surprising news. It began with the unhappy death of Frank's mother. Then shortly after, Mrs Weston had something more to tell her.

'Emma my dear, I have some very bad news,' said Mrs Weston. 'I don't know how to tell you this but Frank and Jane Fairfax are **engaged**. They have been secretly engaged since Weymouth! It had to be a secret because Mrs Churchill didn't want Frank to marry a girl from a poor family.'

Emma was very surprised, but she remembered Mr Knightley's words. 'So he was right!' she thought to herself.

Then she noticed that Mrs Weston was looking at her strangely, and suddenly she understood.

'Mrs Weston,' cried Emma. 'I know what you are thinking! You think that I am in love with Frank, don't you?'

'Well, yes . . . we thought . . . well, we wanted to believe . . .' began Mrs Weston, but she did not really know what to say.

'Perhaps at first I thought I was,' said Emma. 'But we both soon realized that we weren't in love. We were just having fun. But oh dear, what about Jane?' Emma cried. 'What did she think when she saw Frank and me together, flirting all the time!'

Emma remembered the ball and the picnic, and she blushed!

'Oh Emma, I am so relieved that you aren't in love with Frank!' said Mrs Weston. 'I have been so worried about it. But you are right of course. I don't know what Jane thought.'

'I can't forgive Frank for this!' said Emma angrily.

'Emma, I know that it's hard, but try not to be cross,' said Mrs Weston. 'Let's wait for him to explain. Mr Churchill has said yes to the wedding, so we must think of that now.'

'Oh no, and what about poor Harriet!' thought Emma while she walked home. 'I can't believe that we have made the same mistake again!'

engaged when two people agree that they are going to marry

READING CHECK

What do they say?

2 'Frank's going to marry Jane Fairfax!'

1 'All right, everyone. Let's all say two clever things and three silly things.'

3 'How could you be so rude to Miss Bates?'

5 'I'm bored. Can you think of a game to play?'

6 'Jane is going to work as a governess.'

4 'I can't say clever things, but I can say silly things,'

7 'Oh, no! What will Harriet say about this?'

8 'Oh, but I'm not in love with Frank!'

9 'The difficult thing for you, Miss Bates, will be to say no more than three silly things.'

a Emma says to Frank, ...5..
b Frank says, ...
c ..... answers Miss Bates.
d Emma then says, ...
e Later Mr Knightley angrily asks Emma, ...
f The next day at her house Miss Bates tells Emma, ...
g Mrs Weston tells Emma, ...
h Emma quickly says to Mrs Weston, ...
i ..... thinks Emma on her way home.

WORD WORK

flirt OFFERED ENGAGED forgive ASHAMED PLEASED tears exactly vain

Complete Emma's diary with words from the hill.

I am (a) .... ashamed .... when I think of the bad things I did during the picnic at Box Hill! Why am I so (b) ...., always thinking that I am the best-looking and the cleverest? Why did I (c) .... with Frank, talking so playfully and smiling so often. I hope that Jane can (d) .... me and agree to forget my silly words. When I learnt that she and Frank were secretly (e) .... all those months ago in Weymouth, and were sure to marry, I felt terrible! My eyes filled with (f) .... Mr Knightley was (g) .... right when he said that Frank loved Jane and I didn't believe him. He (h) .... me help and I turned away from it. Why don't I listen to him more often? At least he looked (i) .... with me after I went to visit Miss Bates to say sorry for being rude to her. Oh dear!

GUESS WHAT

What happens in the next chapter? Tick the boxes.

		Yes	No
a	Harriet is very sad that Frank is marrying Jane.	☐	☐
b	Emma feels strange when Harriet tells her who she loves.	☐	☐
c	Emma realizes that she is in love with someone.	☐	☐
d	Mr Knightley isn't in love with anybody.	☐	☐
e	Jane and Emma become friends.	☐	☐
f	Harriet decides to marry.	☐	☐
g	Emma never marries.	☐	☐

CHAPTER 8

Wonderful news

Just after Emma arrived home, she was surprised to see Harriet walk through the door. 'Well Emma, have you heard about Frank and Jane?' asked Harriet excitedly.

'You know?' said Emma, looking surprised.

'Yes, Mr Weston has just told me. I didn't know that they were engaged. Isn't it exciting?' replied Harriet, smiling.

Emma was **confused**. Why was Harriet so cheerful?

'Harriet, I don't understand. I thought that you would be **upset** to hear this news. I thought . . . well . . . that you and Frank . . . '

'What do you mean Emma?' asked Harriet, 'You don't think that I'm interested in Frank, do you? You *know* who I like! I know that he is much older and richer than me, but . . . *you* told me that perhaps he was the man for me!'

'Harriet,' cried Emma. 'You don't mean Mr Knightley, do you?'

'Why yes, of course I do!' replied Harriet.

'But . . . when we talked of it, I thought that you meant Frank – because he rescued you from the gypsies,' said Emma.

'Of course I didn't mean Frank, Emma! I was talking about Mr Knightley. Don't you remember how he rescued me at the ball?' said Harriet looking surprised. 'And since then, he has been so kind and attentive to me, I am sure that he feels the same about me as I feel about him.'

Emma remembered seeing them together at Donwell Abbey, and again at Hartfield after her visit to Miss Bates. Why did she not notice that Harriet was in love with him before?

'And perhaps Mr Knightley really loves Harriet,' she thought unhappily.

It was all too much for Emma. The **idea** of Harriet and

confused not understanding something clearly

upset unhappy

idea a plan or a new thought

Mr Knightley being in love and perhaps marrying! Mr Knightley was *her* special friend. She could not think of him with Harriet!

It was all too much for Emma.

Then Emma suddenly realized something.

'I never knew it until now, but I believe *I* am in love with Mr Knightley!' she thought in surprise. 'Oh, this is terrible! What shall I do?'

'I now realize how vain and selfish I have been,' she thought. 'All this time I have tried to find Harriet a husband, and I never thought about what *she* wanted. First, I stopped her from marrying Mr Martin, then I wanted her to marry Mr Elton, and finally I decided that she loved Frank! I always thought I knew best!'

Emma began to feel very ashamed of herself.

'I told Harriet that she was too good for Mr Martin and to look for someone better. If she loves Mr Knightley now, then I can only blame myself,' she thought unhappily. 'And it is clear that Mr Knightley doesn't love *me*. He is always cross with me for something.' And she remembered his angry words to her about Mr Martin and Miss Bates.

Emma went to bed tired and unhappy, but she could not sleep.

The next day, when she woke up, she felt **lonely** and **depressed**, so she went for a walk in the garden. She was busy thinking about everything when, to her surprise, Mr Knightley arrived!

Emma tried to be calm. They walked together for a little while but Mr Knightley was quiet, and Emma was unhappy.

'Mr Knightley,' she said, trying to smile and to sound cheerful. 'We have had some news since you have been in London. We will soon have a wedding in Highbury.'

Mr Knightley looked kindly at her unhappy face. 'I know Emma. I have heard,' he said softly. 'I can see that you are very unhappy, but believe me, Emma, in time you will forget Frank.' And he took her hand.

'Oh Mr Knightley,' said Emma looking surprised. 'You think that I am in love with Frank, too, don't you? Please believe me. We were both vain and silly, but Frank and I have never been in love. We are just friends,' she explained.

'Is this really true?' asked Mr Knightley, 'I thought . . .'

'I know.' said Emma unhappily. 'Everyone thought . . .'

'I have something that I need to say to you.'

'Then I have something that I need to say to you,' said Mr Knightley, looking at her with hope in his eyes.

'Emma, we are friends, and I believe that you understand me better than anyone in the world.' He stopped and took her hand again. 'My dearest Emma, I love you and I have always loved you. Will you marry me?'

Emma could not believe what she was hearing. Mr Knightley loved *her*, not Harriet! He forgave her for being vain and silly. Emma was so happy that she could not speak, but finally she found her voice.

'Yes, of course I will marry you, Mr Knightley. I love you more than anyone!'

'Oh Emma, all this time I thought that you were in love with Frank! I have been *so* jealous of him,' he explained. 'After the picnic I was so **convinced** of your love for him that I decided to leave Highbury.'

Emma blushed, but Mr Knightley smiled kindly, and she could not feel embarrassed for long. She was too happy. Later, they went inside and had tea with Emma's father, but they decided not to tell him the news that they were engaged yet.

'Oh, but how can I tell Harriet?' thought Emma when she was alone. 'I can't see her and *not* tell her the truth!'

So the next day, Emma wrote a letter to her sister Isabella and asked her to invite Harriet to London for a few days. She knew that Harriet would love a holiday, and she thought that it would give her time to think. She loved her friend and did not want to hurt her.

The same day, Mrs Weston brought Emma a letter from Frank. He was very, very sorry for not telling Emma the truth about himself and Jane. Emma still felt cross with him, but she could not stay cross for long.

'I want us to be friends again,' she thought. 'But I also want to be friends with Jane.'

convinced sure

She decided to visit Jane, but on the day that she went, Mrs Elton was at the house too, and Emma felt that she couldn't speak freely in front of her. When it was time for Emma to go, Jane took her to the door herself.

'Emma, let me explain,' said Jane, talking **confidentially**. 'Please forgive me for being cold and unfriendly to you all this time. But I couldn't be your friend and *not* tell you the truth about Frank and me. It had to be a secret, so I wasn't friendly to Frank **in public** either. He didn't like that, so he spent all his time with you – to make me jealous! After that, I was so unhappy about my new job as a governess with Mrs Smallridge, far away from Highbury and from Frank. I'm sorry, Emma. I really don't like secrets.'

'But Jane, *I* am sorry. Please let's just forget everything and be friends,' said Emma, and they both smiled.

Yes, it was time to be friends, but Emma knew that she could not be happy until Harriet knew about Mr Knightley.

One day, shortly after that, while Harriet was still in London, Mr Knightley told Emma something very surprising.

'Emma, I am afraid I have something to tell you which you won't **approve of**. I have had a letter from Robert Martin.'

Emma looked confused and wondered what he meant.

'He has been in London for a few days now, and while he was there he met Harriet again. 'Well, Emma,' he said, looking worried, 'he and Harriet are now engaged!'

'Oh Mr Knightley, this is wonderful news!' cried Emma.

Now Mr Knightley looked confused.

'I made a terrible mistake trying to matchmake for Harriet,' explained Emma. 'I now know that it was wrong of me. Mr Martin is a good man, and I believe Harriet has always loved him. I just hope that they can forgive me for always thinking I know best,' she said truthfully.

confidentially secretly

in public in front of other people

approve of to think that something is good

52

Mr Knightley looked at her and smiled. How he loved his beautiful Emma!

When Frank came to Highbury, he and Jane visited Emma. They were all embarrassed at first, but Frank was soon laughing and talking about their wedding in London.

Harriet also blushed when she saw Emma again, and they remembered their conversation about Mr Knightley.

'I was very silly Emma,' said Harriet. 'I know now that I have only ever loved Mr Martin.'

So there were two weddings in Highbury that year – first Harriet's and Mr Martin's and then, a month later, Emma's and Mr Knightley's – and after that Emma decided never to matchmake again.

So there were two weddings in Highbury.

READING CHECK

Correct the mistakes in these sentences.

a Harriet is ~~worried~~ *pleased* that Frank is marrying Jane.

b Harriet tells Emma that she wants to marry Frank.

c Emma realizes that she is really in love with Frank.

d Emma feels embarrassed about trying to find a husband for Miss Bates.

e Emma thinks that perhaps Mr Knightley is in love with Miss Bates.

f Mr Knightley asks Emma to leave him.

g Emma wants to hurt Harriet.

h Miss Bates decides to marry Robert Martin.

WORD WORK

Use the words in the wedding cake to complete the sentences.

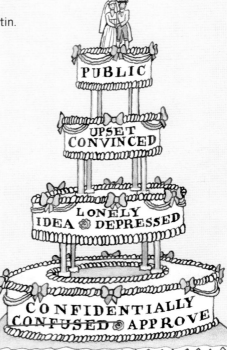

PUBLIC

UPSET
CONVINCED

LONELY
IDEA ❀ DEPRESSED

CONFIDENTIALLY
CONFUSED ❀ APPROVE

a 'I'm feeling *confused*.'

'I know, dear. You don't have any .... of where you are.'